THE SEXUAL ECSTASY WORKBOOK

D1568431

THE SEXUAL ECSTASY WORKBOOK

THE PATH OF SKYDANCING® TANTRA

MARGOT ANAND

with

Philip Duane Johncock

Illustrations from *The Art of Sexual Ecstasy* and *The Art of Sexual Magic*
Exercises from *The Art of Sexual Ecstasy*

JEREMY P. TARCHER/PENGUIN
A MEMBER OF
PENGUIN GROUP (USA) INC.
NEW YORK

JEREMY P. TARCHER/PENGUIN
Published by the Penguin Group
www.penguin.com
Penguin Group (USA) Inc., 375 Hudson Street, New York, New York 10014, USA
Penguin Group (Canada), 10 Alcorn Avenue, Toronto, Ontario, Canada M4V 3B2 (a division of Pearson Penguin Canada Inc.) •
Penguin Books Ltd, 80 Strand, London WC2R 0RL, England • Penguin Ireland, 25 St Stephen's Green, Dublin 2, Ireland (a division
of Penguin Books Ltd) • Penguin Group (Australia), 250 Camberwell Road, Camberwell, Victoria 3124, Australia (a division of
Pearson Australia Group Pty Ltd) • Penguin Books India Pvt Ltd, 11 Community Centre, Panchsheel Park, New Delhi–110 017, India •
Penguin Group (NZ), Cnr Airborne and Rosedale Roads, Albany, Auckland 1310, New Zealand (a division of Pearson New Zealand
Ltd) • Penguin Books (South Africa) (Pty) Ltd, 24 Sturdee Avenue, Rosebank, Johannesburg 2196, South Africa

Penguin Books Ltd, Registered Offices: 80 Strand, London WC2R 0RL, England

Most Tarcher/Penguin books are available at special quantity discounts for bulk purchase for sales promotions, premiums, fund-raising,
and educational needs. Special books or book excerpts also can be created to fit specific needs. For details, write
Penguin Group (USA) Inc. Special Markets, 375 Hudson Street, New York, NY 10014.

While the authors have made every effort to provide accurate telephone numbers and Internet addresses at the time of publication,
neither the publisher nor the authors assume any responsibility for errors, or for changes that occur after publication.

ISBN 1-58542-397-1

Printed in the United States of America
1   3   5   7   9   10   8   6   4   2

This book is printed on acid-free paper. ♾

Book design by Tanya Maiboroda

CONTENTS

INTRODUCTION

Have you ever been at a concert and marveled at the beauty of the sound, the music seeming to lift you off your chair, the instruments so perfectly tuned that each note emerged from the others, distinct yet perfectly blended: one body of sound, created as if no player were separate from the whole orchestra?

Such concerts lift our spirits and cleanse our souls. So it should be with lovemaking.

Lovers are the instruments and the players all at once in a private symphony of love. This means that instruments must be tuned and players warmed up and limber, before the concert starts. Otherwise, love makes cacophonous noise—and no harmony at all.

When lovers know how to move gracefully, breathe deeply, relax fully, and look into each other's eyes and through the eyes into their united souls, the pure music of love rings forth like a symphonic revelation. Such presence in body, heart, and soul is what we need in order to engage in love as a journey of harmonious connection, erotic devotion, and spiritual awakening. This is what the path of SkyDancing Tantra is about.

The Sexual Ecstasy Workbook presents a summary of the Love and Ecstasy Training, an aspect of Tantra that teaches us to follow with awareness what gives us joy, and by doing so, open the door to spirit. It presents a proven method: SkyDancing Tantra, which helps partners to create a deep resonance before actually engaging in sex. It teaches the language of bliss. Learn it, and you will learn the attitude of openhearted commitment that will allow you to realize your full potential as a lover and as a human being.

I was recently invited to speak to a gathering of Fortune 500 CEOs. For the most part, these people appeared to be in loving relationships with their spouses. Yet everyone, without exception, had one major complaint: "No time to cultivate good sex." This complaint was confirmed by a recent issue of *Newsweek* with the cover story "No Sex, Please, We're Married: Are Stress, Kids and Work Killing Romance?"

The sad facts are well-known:

- 44 million Americans are mired in low-sex or no-sex marriages.
- Half of American marriages end in divorce.
- 75 percent of couples are dissatisfied with their sex lives.
- 66 percent of American women do not experience orgasm during sex.
- Men's sex education comes mostly from the locker room.
- Most people experience less than 10 percent of their pleasure potential.

The Sexual Ecstasy Workbook is the perfect practical guide for the countless lovers who complain that sexual harmony is so easily broken, that love, rather than being pure bliss, is more like walking through a minefield—where at any moment a false move can turn off enthusiasm and snuff out any chance for orgasmic success.

Here are some of the problematic situations you will learn how to successfully manage:

- She is turned on and wants to make love, but she is too shy to express it.
- He wants her but she seems busy, so he doesn't dare interrupt and ask.
- The children walk in and disrupt the mood.
- The world—in the form of ringing cell phones, beeping pagers, droning television, to-do lists, domestic duties, and so on—prevents the focused intimacy that is at the core of bliss.
- He "lands" before she has even had the time to "take off," then goes to sleep; she is frustrated, resentful, and bottled up.
- Fear and resistance prevent feeling much of anything.
- Awkwardness—not knowing how to caress each other sensuously—turns lovemaking into a burdensome chore.
- Shyness prevents us from showing ourselves freely in front of the other and prevents us from fully cultivating erotic pleasure.

The Sexual Ecstasy Workbook presents a user-friendly, easy-access, step-by-step method for connecting more deeply with yourself, your ecstatic potential, your erotic goals, and your ability to appreciate yourself and your partner. It's the tool you need if you do not want to sacrifice your love life to the stresses of a busy schedule.

Great lovemaking doesn't necessarily happen when a man's penis enters a woman's vagina. Far from it. Intercourse should be the glorious peak of an event, a sacred activity in which lovers, like master musicians, take time to tune in and warm up. Tune up the heart, the breath, and the commitment to love, so that you can be fully present and attentive to your partner in the precious intimacy of each moment.

Great lovemaking happens when:

- You have created a safe space in which you can let go and open your heart.
- The woman feels her man's presence and commitment to her well-being.
- The man feels his woman's openness and acceptance.

- You feel you deserve a good orgasm—because you love yourself—and you're willing to do what it takes to make it happen.
- You keep yourself in good shape so you can practice different love positions comfortably.
- You learn and practice the three keys to orgasmic power.
- Each lover resonates with the other, and each knows how to circulate energy through his or her own heart and body and back to the other.

I work with people around the world—more than forty thousand to date—old and young, singles, couples, rich, poor, black and white, heterosexual and gay/lesbian, from many religious and cultural backgrounds. I am always surprised how scared people are of sex. Of course, everyone wants great sex. But too few people dare to take the necessary steps that open the door to better sex. Too few people even know the steps to take in the first place. Too many people fail to experiment by taking a romantic weekend away or by trying a new lovemaking style. Too many are too tired to go to a workshop or too embarrassed to consult a therapist. We're often too busy and impatient to take the time to really learn about sex or communicate about delicate sexual issues. So, instead, we stay stuck in our old unsatisfying patterns. Maybe we don't think we are "good enough" or "attractive enough" to deserve great sex. Well, these unproductive attitudes and situations happen to all of us from time to time—and to some of us all of the time.

When I first decided to train in the skills of extended sexual orgasm, I noticed a huge resistance in myself—I always had more urgent things to do. So I had to learn not to listen to my mind. My partner and I took the time we needed to train ourselves in the skills of love. We made appointments to practice, and we honored our appointments. In the end, it paid off in spades. Instead of needing an hour or more to reach orgasm, I found I needed only ten minutes and could have many orgasms in the space of half an hour. My partner knew exactly what to do because I took the time to explain to him everything I wanted, and he took the time to listen with an open heart and a commitment to do it the right way for me. Of course, I did the same for him.

The skills in *The Sexual Ecstasy Workbook* take practice. I guarantee that you will be richly rewarded for the time and effort you put forth. You'll learn the language of SkyDancing Tantra: a set of delightful skills to cultivate at your own pace. Ideally, I recommend that you practice these skills one to two hours a week. Surely an ecstatic sex life is worth this much of your time! Think of it as fitness training—for love and ecstasy!

More than forty thousand people worldwide have participated in the Love and Ecstasy Training and studied SkyDancing Tantra. Many more have studied it through my books—*The Art of Sexual Ecstasy* and *The Art of Sexual Magic.* The method works. It's that simple. All you need is a commitment to practice on a regular basis.

I suggest you set aside one evening a week for practice. I recommend Wednesday, because it's the middle of the week, when many of us feel tired and overwhelmed by stress. At such times, SkyDancing Tantra and *The Sexual Ecstasy Workbook* are there to give you a boost. Try to leave work by six P.M. Between six and eight P.M., shower, have a light meal, and create a beautiful, safe space in which you and your partner can practice. From eight to ten or eleven P.M., practice a skill, or several, from this workbook. Your repeated commitment to loving each other with awareness and erotic devotion is guaranteed to bring healing and delight to your life.

If you are on your own and have no partner, you can do most of the practices with yourself in front of a mirror, or with your Inner Lover, whom you'll soon meet if you haven't already. Remember, loving yourself is the prerequisite to loving and being loved by another.

These practices work for both heterosexual and homosexual couples. Many of them work well outside a sexual context altogether, enhancing the quality of relationships within families and for friends, too.

If you're in a helping profession—counselor, nurse, doctor, or therapist—this workbook offers powerful resources to support your clients in their inner growth and to help them get started on the path to integrated sexual awareness.

This workbook is designed to stand alone, but you can deepen your practice by consulting my other books, as well as the DVD/video *The Art of Sexual Ecstasy.* They're a support that can serve as a reminder for people who have already studied my work somewhat, but also a user-friendly introduction for anyone just beginning the exciting journey on the path to ecstatic sexuality.

Now take a deep breath and imagine your erotic sensations begining to flow throughout your whole body. Say to yourself, "I am worth it." And when you say it, feel your voice color your sensations with the potential for bliss.

Now you're ready to start the practice of SkyDancing Tantra.

Bon voyage!

Instead of having sex, try making love. Sex is "work" when your heart isn't in it. Forget about sex. Just play first. Dance, sing, read to each other, make up poems, be tender, open your hearts, communicate. Let sex be the crowning of this exchange. The "work" or effort, if any, is in learning self-acceptance, developing real self-love, paying attention to your breath, befriending your body, and communicating with each other about delicate subjects such as sexual fears and fantasies. Don't count on sex to be the door to intimacy. It's the other way around: first develop intimacy skills. Then make love to enjoy them.

—MARGOT ANAND

CHAPTER I

GET
STARTED

EIGHT STEPS TO MASTERY

Here are eight easy steps to mastering sexual ecstasy and the fifteen SkyDancing Tantra skills presented in this workbook:

1. *Scan* the contents page to get a feel for the terrain you will be covering.
2. *Read* "What Is SkyDancing Tantra?" and "Seven SkyDancing Attitudes." These sections are designed to help you deepen your experience of sexual ecstasy and mastery of the Sky-Dancing Tantra skills.
3. *Set your intention and commitment* by completing and signing the form in this workbook. Doing so will jump-start your learning process and build a solid foundation for your exploration.

4. *Read "Guidelines"* for ways to prepare your body, mind, and spirit for sexual ecstasy and mastering SkyDancing Tantra skills.
5. *Pick up* a copy of *The Art of Sexual Ecstasy: The Path of Sacred Sexuality for Western Lovers* by Margot Anand (Jeremy P. Tarcher/Putnam, 1989). It is a great supplemental resource to this workbook.
6. *Briefly write down* in this workbook your experiences at the end of each practice session. It would also be helpful to keep a special SkyDancing journal, where you write about your impressions and experiences in more depth.
7. *Imagine how to creatively integrate* sexual awareness and SkyDancing Tantra skills into your lovemaking and into your life, too.
8. *Watch* the DVD/video film *The Art of Sexual Ecstasy.*

WHAT IS SKYDANCING TANTRA?

Tantra, like Yoga and Zen, is a path to enlightenment. Born thousands of years ago in India, Tantra later spread to Tibet, Nepal, and China, where it was known as the Tao of Love. Once the cherished practice of Asian nobility, it became known as the Yoga of Love. Like other forms of yoga, the practice of SkyDancing Tantra offers peace of mind while it both relaxes and energizes the body. SkyDancing Tantra enables one to overcome feelings of separation and experience a sense of union.

SkyDancing Tantra presents the Tantric paradigm of the East through methods easily accessible to the Western culture and lifestyle. Westernized largely through the work of Margot Anand, author of *The Art of Sexual Ecstasy, The Art of Sexual Magic, The Art of Everyday Ecstasy,* and *Sexual Ecstasy: The Art of Orgasm,* the ancient spirit of Tantra has been combined with the recent discoveries in clinical sexology, as well as humanistic and transpersonal psychology.

SkyDancing Tantra relaxes the body, opens the heart, and clears the mind. When integration of body, heart, and mind has taken place, you are ready for a new sexual experience in which physical pleasure becomes a delight of the heart and an ecstasy of the spirit. When practiced with a partner, SkyDancing Tantra contributes to a healthy, loving relationship.

SkyDancing Tantra skills are powerful, healing, and effective. They have been taught successfully by licensed SkyDancing instructors to more than forty thousand people worldwide.

SkyDancing is an ancient metaphor for achieving ecstatic states. SkyDancing Tantra is the ability to integrate these ecstatic states into your lovemaking and your life, so that love and sexuality can be experienced as a flow, a joyful celebration, a healing meditation.

Margot Anand received the practices of SkyDancing Tantra while in deep meditation, and through direct transmission and inner vision of the steps of the method. Margot studied many holistic traditions, such as Taoism, Buddhism, Hinduism, and Native American teachings. SkyDancing Tantra distills these traditions into the Love and Ecstasy Training (L.E.T.) that is accessible to current generations and the Western world. It is a blending of the ancient with modern techniques of bioenergetics, NLP, visualization, meditation, yoga, effective communication skills, ritual, massage, magic, and other heart-centered methods.

The path of SkyDancing Tantra, as developed by Margot Anand and taught by teachers licensed in the SkyDancing methods, helps your body to be free of tensions, your heart to be open and trusting, and your mind to develop the psychic skills of visualization, imagination, transparency, and meditation. The goal is to celebrate the essence of who we are and our experience of ecstasy and wholeness.

SkyDancing Tantra teaches us to honor ourselves and each other as we are. We were born ecstatic. Ecstasy is our very nature. It is not to be found outside; it is already within us. As ecstatic beings, already perfect, our responsibility is to reclaim and live loving and ecstatic lives.

Developing our ecstatic potential in sex is a wonderful place to start.

The Buddha, Vajrasattva, and his Consort, The Dakini: Great Dignity, in blissful union, are dancing in the sky. This is the logo of SkyDancing Tantra.

4

SEVEN SkyDancing Attitudes

Experience with more than forty thousand people throughout the world has revealed a lot about how we open to Tantric teachings and how we expand the experience of sexual ecstasy in our lives. We have found that a certain mind-set, which we affectionately refer to as Sky-Dancing Attitudes, can enhance your experience of learning Tantra.

We invite you to read and try on, like a new set of clothes, all seven attitudes. We are confident that your experience of sexual ecstasy will be even more expansive, magical, and transformative.

Generate Safety!

Like everybody else, no matter where you are, before you're willing to open yourself fully and be vulnerable, you need to feel safe. For your exploration of sexual ecstasy to be a positive experience, trust is a must.

This book provides you with tools to create a safe space to explore sexual ecstasy, but ultimately you are responsible for generating your own safety. We request that you commit to taking full responsibility for generating your own safety.

One way to begin is to periodically ask yourself, "In this moment, what do I need to say or do to feel safe?"

Say this sentence out loud, placing your name in the blank: *I, _____, agree to take full responsibility for generating my own safety.*

Celebrate Sexuality and Cultivate Pleasure!

Create an atmosphere of expectancy and excitement. The spontaneous, sensual, vibrant aspects of your true essence are joyously waiting for you just around the bend, within each experience and moment. We're here to encourage you as you discover, express, and celebrate your ecstatic self through pleasure and delight. SkyDancing Tantra is a celebration, not a therapy. SkyDancing Tantrikas—those who practice SkyDancing Tantra—consider themselves celebration partners whose job it is to:

- Celebrate the inherent perfection of our ecstatic natures
- Learn how to enjoy our sexuality and life as a dance
- Provide a safe space in which spontaneous, sensual, and vibrant aspects of ourselves can be discovered and find expression

The SkyDancing approach assumes that sexual healing, as well as personal growth, can take place through pleasure and delight much more easily and enjoyably than by focusing on pain or problems, which is often the approach used in many forms of therapy.

Say this sentence out loud: *I, _____, am willing to celebrate fully my sexual expression and delight.*

Suffering and struggle, even pain, are optional, although often more familiar and socially acceptable. Develop your pleasurability, the precious ability to be totally and unconditionally receptive to pleasure. Create time in your busy schedule for pleasure.

Say this sentence out loud: *I, _____, create time to cultivate pleasure in my life and increase my pleasurability.*

Be Childlike!

Play, have outrageous fun, laugh, use your imagination, be childlike, innocent. Experience each Tantric practice anew and fresh. Find that place within where wonder and curiosity reside, and invite that childlike wonder and curiosity into your exploration. Leave your judge, critic, and worrier personas at the door. You can always pick them up on the way out when you are done.

Say this sentence out loud: *I, _____, invite childlike qualities, such as wonder, curiosity, and play, into my sexual awareness and exploration.*

View Sexuality as Energy!

Sexuality is first a matter of energy, pure, guilt-free, organic, good vibrations. Often we over-lay our experience of our innate sexuality with layers of parental and societal programming, guilt, shame, and fear. SkyDancing Tantra views sexual energy as the movement of life. Sky-Dancing Tantra tools are designed to allow people to cultivate sexual ecstasy and awaken their ecstatic selves independently from intercourse. Sexual healing, relaxing in high states of arousal, expanding sexual pleasure, opening to whole-body orgasms—these and more can be learned in a safe, supportive environment without nudity or genital contact.

First, create a safe environment in which to learn. Then, agree with yourself that you are willing to move beyond your previous conditioning and programming around sex to see your sexuality as an emerging energetic experience.

Say this sentence out loud: *I, _____, am ready to embrace my full sexual energy.*

Surrender and Melt!

Discover ways to relax your body and mind. The word *surrender* means to melt (render) into that which is higher than your self. True surrender is a conscious choice made from free will. Surrender and melt into your heart. Surrender and melt into the ecstatic vibrations in your body. Relax into pleasure. Surrender and melt into love, ecstasy, and wholeness.

Say this sentence out loud: *I, _____, surrender and melt into deep pleasure, love, and ecstasy.*

Connect Sex with Heart and Spirit!

Very often, people look at sexuality as something that's kept in the closet, as something you do separate from your spiritual path. They say, "Sex isn't spiritual." However, SkyDancing Tantra can actually enhance your existing spiritual practices. You can harness this very creative, basic, profound, and vital force, the root of all life in a way that is like a prayer, a meditation, a devotion.

This means that sitting in front of you in a partner is an image of God, an aspect of the Divine, and they themselves are made in the image of God. You can respect and honor your partner as an aspect of the Divinity rather than see your partner as an object of your lust or desire.

This also means that your body and your spirit do not have to remain separate. Your body can be a container for your spirit, something that you honor and hold sacred.

Say this sentence to yourself out loud: *I, _____, honor my sex, heart, and spirit. I honor the divinity within myself and others.*

Appreciate Your Inner Rebel!

Tantra was born out of a rebellion against old beliefs. Pioneering something new often means rebelling against old beliefs. Each one of us has within us an inner rebel who wants to be free, who wants to defy entrenched traditions, who wants to do whatever it wants, and especially not do what someone else wants it to do. Instead of making this inner rebel wrong, let's open space for the rebel to be present and acknowledged as a pioneer.

The rebel may appear when we don't want to do an activity or participate fully when a partner wants to. Yet acknowledging the inner rebel will allow you to resonate with what's true and allow you to recommit to move beyond your own resistances and patterns of self-sabotage. Be a pioneer. Harness the power of your inner rebel and become a full-fledged pattern breaker.

Say this sentence to yourself out loud: *I, _____, acknowledge and appreciate my inner rebel.*

Keep these seven SkyDancing Tantra attitudes fresh in your mind as you practice the skills in this workbook. Review them periodically. Doing so will deepen your experiences and make learning the SkyDancing Tantra skills easier.

COMMITMENT AND INTENTION

Experience shows that deep and lasting transformation happens when you are willing to make a series of simple, yet profound commitments and declare an intention for what you really want. We invite you to read, commit to, and sign the following Commitment to Sexual Ecstasy. Then declare your intention.

Commitment to Sexual Ecstasy

I am a discovering ecstatic being. To learn and experience more joy in my life, I now commit myself to the following self-nurturing agreements:

I understand that I am undertaking an intensive encounter with my own sexuality. I would like my learning experiences to be easeful and gentle. I understand that this exploration may raise issues and emotions for me to deal with. I agree to take 100 percent responsibility for my well-being. I agree to seek help or professional assistance, if necessary.

I commit to cultivate pleasure, intimacy, and ecstasy and to move beyond unconscious habits and tendencies to get lost in pain, old character patterns, childhood wounds, and separateness.

I am open to loving and accepting myself more.

I agree to practice SkyDancing Tantra in a way that is safe and loving for me.

Signature _____   *Date* _____

Intention

What is your intention or purpose for embarking on this journey into your sexual ecstasy? What do you really want? What would you like to get out of this workbook and the skills you learn?

Take a few moments to write down your intention(s). Remember, specific intentions bring greater results.

_____

_____

_____

_____

_____

GUIDELINES

We invite you to read and use these guidelines as you begin your Tantric practices.

Honor Your Body as Your Temple

Take care of your physical, emotional, and mental well-being. Rest is very important. Watch your energy level, and don't overdo it. Find moments each day to be quiet, to rest, and to nurture yourself. Find time to go both inside and outside.

- *Drink plenty of water.* Ecstasy is electricity, and water is an excellent conductor. Drinking water will help keep you grounded and clear, and it will speed up the clearing of toxins from your body.

❧ *Use personal hygiene.* Please come to your practices having brushed your teeth and washed your hands. Wear fresh clothes and shower often. Feel clean, fresh, perfumed, and attractive.

The importance of honoring your body temple and personal hygiene struck me (Margot) the strongest when I arrived in a temple in India, the ashram of a Tantric master I was visiting. I saw the guardian of the temple, Suresh Ananda—whose name means Guardian of Bliss.

He was sweeping the floor, opening the windows, and giving an offering of saffron rice in front of each of the statues of the deities. He was dressing the deities. He was sprinkling them with coconut milk and putting fresh garlands of flowers around their necks. He was lighting sticks of incense in front of them.

I saw this temple as a metaphor of our bodies. If we treat the temple well—that is, we clean it and freshen everything—then spirit will be naturally drawn to this abode, to extend its blessings to whomever is coming to visit.

On the other hand, if the temple is not tended, is full of junk food and old crumpled papers, the garbage hasn't been emptied, flowers have faded, and food is rotten, then who would want to come to that temple and smell mildew and bad odors?

So I realized that is the same way we treat our physical "temple." Our body is our temple. If we treat it well, then our spirit is going to be attracted to the temple; it will want to shine and give its gifts.

If we don't treat our temple well, filling it full of dust, mold, too much sugar, junk food, cigarettes, and such, then our spirits will have no place to feel welcome.

Say Yes to Whatever Comes Up

SkyDancing Tantra says that everything you experience, regardless of what it is or whether it is judged good or bad, is an opportunity to be creative, an opportunity for healing and learning. Your experience, whatever it might be and however it might look, is perfect for you.

Whatever feelings, thoughts, body sensations arise, say yes to them. Befriend them. Even resistances. Instead of beating yourself up for resisting, say, "Yes. I am resisting," then examine your resistances. What are they protecting you from? Do you really need them? Is moving into the resistance offering you a chance to move beyond it?

SkyDancing Tantra welcomes all your experiences, all of you.

CHAPTER 2

SKYDANCING
TANTRA SKILLS

Create a Safe Space

Benefits

- ⚘ Create a container for energy
- ⚘ Create a space where you feel safe and where you can safely explore your ecstatic potential
- ⚘ Use ritual to clear mental and physical space and feel more present

Purpose

- ⚘ To create a space in which SkyDancing Tantra practices can be explored in privacy, without interruption, and in a distinctly separate context from everyday living

Summary

You can create a safe space alone or with a partner.

First, walk three times counterclockwise around the space. Say out loud all negative qualities that you want to remove from this space. Make sure that any windows and doors are open. Recite a symbolic declaration, with gestures, as you throw out the negative energies, one at a time. Say, *I remove* _____ *[sadness, self-doubt, jealousy, impatience, stress, judgments, pain] from this space.*

Second, walk in the other direction—clockwise—three times. Make sounds with instruments like drums, tambourines, or bells, if you have any. Call forth the individual positive energies that you want to bring in. Say, *I call forth* _____ *[joy, patience, conviviality, eroticism, compassion, orgasmic power, love] into this space.* With your arms, using deep breathing, make gestures that bring new energies into the space.

Third, face and honor the four directions. Invite in the elements and qualities associated with each direction:

East, fire—spirit and passion

South, water—innocence and love

West, earth—vitality and strength

North, air—clarity and vision

Finally, walk into the space and honor yourself. If you are with a partner, walk into the space together and honor each other. For ideas about honoring, see "Honor Your Partner with a Heart Salutation."

(Modified from pages 65–78 of *The Art of Sexual Ecstasy*.)

Quick Steps

1. Remove the negative. Walk around the space three times counterclockwise, saying out loud the negative qualities that you would like removed: *I remove* _____ *[sadness, self-doubt, jealousy, impatience, stress, judgments, pain] from this space.*

2. Invite in positive. Walk around the space three times clockwise, saying out loud the positive qualities that you would like to invite into the space: *I call forth* _____ *[joy, patience, conviviality, eroticism, compassion, orgasmic power, love] into this space.*

3. Honor the directions and elements. Face and honor each of the four directions (east, fire—spirit and passion; south, water—innocence and love; west, earth—vitality and strength; north, air—clarity and vision).

4. Walk into the space. Honor yourself and your partner. (See the Heart Salutation, pages 31–32.)

SkyDancing Attitudes

- ꙮ Generate safety
- ꙮ Be childlike

Your Experience

Describe your experience creating a safe space:

_____

_____

_____

_____

_____

_____

_____

_____

_____

TIP: ELIMINATE DISTRACTIONS

No one likes to enter a space of focused attention to share intimate concerns and then be interrupted by the jarring ring of a telephone. Put your love and care into creating a safe space to practice. Keep the space clean and fresh. Eliminate distractions by unplugging the phone, turning off cell phones, scheduling practices at times when you won't be disturbed, putting up DO NOT DISTURB signs, and so on.

> ### TIP: TRANSFORM TRIGGERING
>
> Very often in a love relationship, one or the other partner comes to a point where they get triggered by something they feel the other has done "wrong." In fact, what is likely happening is that what the other does elicits a contraction in their being because it reminds them of a wounded childhood moment or a previous bad relationship. It's a wound from the past that is still imprinted in their body-mind in the present moment.
>
> So the particular practice of creating a safe space allows the partners to find an intermediary step in which each says, "I commit to using a skillful means to give myself space and time to have more choice and discrimination as to my responses during this practice. So that even if I get contracted, I don't follow the usual temptation to immediately interpret the contraction as something 'bad' and make my partner wrong. It's really not you [my partner] who is at fault. I am being triggered, and I can become aware that I have a choice as to how I respond."
>
> The safe space has a powerful healing effect. It is a support through concrete gestures, visioning, invocation voice, body, movement, and visualization to help create a possibility to respond to life, to one's partner, with awareness, in a conscious and loving way.

Homeplay

- *Create a list of objects.* Create a list of objects you would include in your safe space. Here are some examples: power objects of personal significance (such as a stone, a crystal, a photo), a beautiful cloth or sheet to cover the ground; pillows, zafus (round Zen meditation pillows), or cushions; blindfolds; candles, incense, essential oils; musical instruments (Tibetan bells, bowls, cymbals, flute, rattles, tambourine, drum, rain stick); fruit or favorite sweets; juice or favorite drinks; feathers, flowers, and silk scarves; massage oils and water-based sexual lubricants; pictures of loved ones and spiritual teachers.

LIST OF OBJECTS

_____   _____

_____   _____

_____   _____

_____   _____

_____   _____

For additional ideas, read pages 65–78 of *The Art of Sexual Ecstasy*
and pages 47–69 of *The Art of Sexual Magic.*

Awaken Your Inner Lover

Benefits

- 🕊 To accept, appreciate, and love yourself
- 🕊 To experience that you are indeed the principal source of your own pleasure
- 🕊 To remember that you deserve love

Purpose

- 🕊 To begin to show that the more self-accepting you are, the more orgasmic you can become

Summary

Read this script to your partner, or record it for yourself on a tape if you practice on your own.

Play soft, relaxing music in the background.

Begin by making yourself comfortable. You may either sit or lie down.

I invite you to begin with deep, relaxed breathing, letting the breath flow deep into your chest and belly and then slowly out. Let the amplifying and cleansing power of the breath support you as you appreciate yourself.

As you close your eyes and take a deep, cleansing breath, for a minute rest one hand on your heart. Imagine that you are entering into a special relationship with yourself, one in which you are both the lover and the beloved. Feel your heart beating. Follow the ebb and flow of the air passing through your nose and the center of your chest, cleansing and relaxing it. Let the breath be easy and gentle. Watch it go in and out, not putting any effort into the breathing, just staying with it.

Now relax your arms and hands by your side, away from your body.

Now let a memory, an image, a feeling arise behind your closed eyes—a visualization of a time in your past when you felt totally loved and supported, cared for, and protected. Perhaps you remember resting in nature, walking outside during a full moon, lying in your lover's arms, listening to beautiful music, receiving the care and guidance of a special teacher.

Feel the joy, the vitality, the gratitude that arises in such moments. Delight in your youthful innocence, vulnerability, and openness.

Wait here for a little while.

When you are immersed in one strong, rewarding image, breathe deeply as you contemplate it. Settle into deep, rhythmic breathing and participate more fully in the remembered scene, filling in as many details as possible. Let the particular colors, sounds, smells, texture, and taste come back to you—the coziness of your mother's embrace, the smell of her hair; the fragrance of the flowers; the softness of your lover's skin.

Let the feelings of that time well up inside your heart. Welcome your feelings. Amplify them. Feel them as intensely and directly as you can.

Immerse yourself even deeper, hold your hands to your heart, allow the feelings connected to the experience to resonate within you. You may feel the joy you felt then, or the quickening of your heartbeat, or a sense of excitement, or being nurtured. Use your breathing to expand this feeling so as to experience it fully, vibrantly. Carry these sensations along the flow of your breath until they quicken the blood and bring the special thrill of the moment flooding back to you again. Let your consciousness be filled with the feeling that everything is easy, flowing, simple.

Allow a word or a phrase to bubble up into your awareness that expresses the sense of well-being and appreciation of yourself that you are feeling right now. Whisper, "It feels good to love me," or "I really enjoy giving myself support." Repeat these positive statements out loud until you feel the pleasure of hearing them.

You are beginning to hear the voice of your Inner Lover. As you say yes to this voice you may be able to see that life is really on your side, willing to support you, teach you, and help you to grow, if only you allow it.

Take a few moments to allow your Inner Lover to whisper words of love and appreciation to you. Allow the words to wash over you, to bathe you in how special you are.

Then, gradually, return to the present moment, letting your breathing slow down. Release the images, memories, and feelings as you exhale, as if they are birds taking off in flight. You have re-membered who you really are—a lovable person. You have met your Inner Lover.

Take a few minutes to write down your experience, the images, thoughts, and feelings. Then, when you are ready, switch roles with your partner. Later, if you choose, you may share your experiences with your partner.

(Modified from pages 55–59 of *The Art of Sexual Ecstasy.*)

SkyDancing Attitudes

- Generate safety
- Be childlike

Quick Steps

1. Play soft, relaxing music.
2. Read (to a partner) or record the script (if done individually).
3. Write your experience.
4. Switch roles, if doing this practice with a partner.

Your Experience

What word bubbled up into your awareness that expressed your sense of well-being? Write down your experience. What images, symbols, feelings emerged for you?

_____

_____

_____

_____

_____

_____

_____

_____

_____

_____

_____

_____

_____

TIP: TAKE CARE

Remember to take care of yourself even in difficult situations.

TIP: VISUALIZE YOUR PARTNER AS INNER LOVER

See your partner as a manifestation of your Inner Lover.

Homeplay

- Write three ways you can meet and awaken your Inner Lover on a regular basis, such as

  Lying in a friend's arms, relaxing, listening to music, with no plans, no intentions
  Getting a luxurious massage
  Dancing and rolling around on the floor
  Taking a longer lunch break

List ways to meet and awaken your inner lover:

1. _____

2. _____

3. _____

For additional ideas, read pages 47–63 of *The Art of Sexual Ecstasy.*

Also available is the CD *The Art of Sexual Ecstasy,* with the Awakening the Inner Lover

practice guided by Margot Anand, and with music by Steven Halpern.

(See Resources for more information.)

Love Your Body

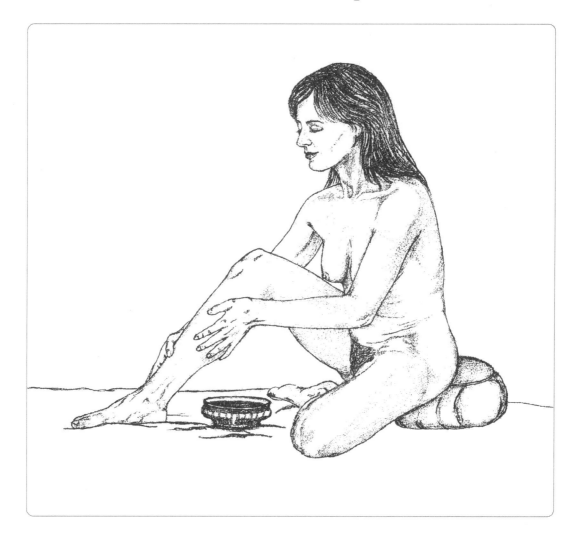

Benefit

- ✎ To recognize that your body, whatever its particular form, is an essential vehicle through which to experience the fullness of your sexual potential

Purpose

- ✎ To be firmly rooted in your body in order to soar to heights of sexual ecstasy
- ✎ To love your body so that it can receive and assimilate subtler and more intense sexual energies

Summary

Do this practice alone.

Stand naked in front of a full-length mirror.

Honor yourself by holding the mirror with your hands folded in front of your heart and bowing.

Take a few deep breaths, observe your body image, and watch your reactions as you do so. If you have any judgments or self-criticism, simply observe them and let them go without becoming identified with them. If you come across certain parts of your body that you cannot easily accept, remember that you are living in this temple, but you are not your body. You are the human spirit that inhabits the temple and is learning about it. Notice and accept that you are judging and criticizing yourself right now, and bring your attention to your breathing. Let go of the thoughts.

Standing or sitting, apply perfume or essences to each part of your body, touching each part with love and care, giving it conscious recognition. As you do so, repeat the following affirmations once:

"Dear feet, you are vehicles of my spirit, and I honor you."
"Dear legs, you are vehicles of my spirit, and I honor you."

"Dear hands, you are vehicles of my spirit, and I honor you."

"Dear arms, you are vehicles of my spirit, and I honor you."

"Dear pelvis, you are a vehicle of my spirit, and I honor you."

"Dear sex (or sexual center), you are a vehicle of my spirit, and I honor you."

"Dear navel and belly, you are vehicles of my spirit, and I honor you."

"Dear heart, you are a vehicle of my spirit, and I honor you."

"Dear mouth and throat, you are vehicles of my spirit, and I honor you."

"Dear eyes, you are vehicles of my spirit, and I honor you."

"Dear ears, you are vehicles of my spirit, and I honor you."

Add any other body parts you need to include into this meditation.

Place the palm of your left hand flat on the middle of your chest. Then lay the palm of your right hand on top of the left. Feel the warmth of your hands flow into your chest. Remain silent for a moment and feel your heart beating and resonating in your hands.

Repeat out loud until you have a really deep sense of resonance: "I appreciate you my body, as a vehicle of my spirit, and I honor you."

Close by bowing and honoring yourself.

(Modified from pages 137–139 of *The Art of Sexual Ecstasy*.)

SkyDancing Attitude

- Connect sex with heart and spirit
- Surrender and melt

Quick Steps

1. Find mirror and perfume.
2. Honor yourself.
3. Honor each part of your body as a vehicle of your spirit.

4. With hands on your heart, honor yourself until you feel a resonance.

5. Conclude by bowing to yourself. (See the Heart Salutation, pages 31–32.)

Your Experience

Describe your experience.

_____

_____

_____

_____

_____

_____

_____

_____

_____

_____

_____

_____

TIP: LOVE THE UNLOVABLE PARTS

Give special attention to the parts of your body that you normally don't like. Love these unlovable parts by talking to them and caressing them.

Homeplay

- ❧ For at least twenty-one days after doing this activity, after you take a shower, while you are applying lotion or oil to your skin, say to yourself out loud, *Hello, _____ [hair, feet, knees, hands]. I appreciate you for _____ [supporting me, giving me flexibility, allowing me to play music]. I honor you.*
- ❧ Stay aware of your body parts throughout the day. Listen to their messages.

For additional ideas, read pages 123–128 and 136–139 of
The Art of Sexual Ecstasy.

Honor Your Partner with a Heart Salutation

Benefits

- ✎ To mark that you are ready to begin or end a Tantric practice
- ✎ To create a complete cycle of energy from the earth to your heart, to your partner, back to your heart, and down to the earth

Purpose

- ✎ To begin and end each Tantric practice with a ritual that communicates "I recognize and honor you from my heart."

Summary

Sit facing your partner for a few minutes, gazing gently into his or her eyes.

If you do this practice alone, you can face a mirror or imagine that you are facing your Inner Lover.

Bring the palms of your hands together and point your fingers down and touch the ground. If you are sitting on a chair, point your fingers toward the earth. Exhale.

With your hands still together, inhale, lift your hands up to your heart, and rest your thumbs against your chest.

Together with your partner, close your eyes. As you exhale, gently bend forward from the waist, keeping your back straight, until your foreheads touch.

Take in the full sense of honor and reverence that this conveys, letting go of all extraneous concerns while you focus on your breathing and your awareness in your heart.

On the next inhale, lean back gently with your back straight, keeping your hands folded against your chest.

With your back straight, exhale and lower your hands to the earth. The palms of your hands are still together, and the tips of your fingers touch the earth.

Open your eyes, look into your partner's eyes, and say, *[Your partner's or Inner Lover's name], I honor you as an aspect of myself* or *I honor you as an aspect of the Divine.*

(Modified from pages 59–62 of *The Art of Sexual Ecstasy.*)

SkyDancing Attitudes

- Generate safety
- Connect sex with heart and spirit
- Surrender and melt

Quick Steps

1. Sit facing partner.
2. Pull energy from earth to heart on inhale.
3. On exhale, bend forward with back straight until your foreheads gently touch.
4. On next inhale, sit back.
5. On last exhale, send energy to earth.
6. Honor your partner as an aspect of the Divine.

Your Experience

Take a moment to write down how this simple activity affected you. Describe what you liked most.

_____

_____

_____

_____

_____

TIP: TOUCH WITH THE HEART

One definition of the word *appreciate* is "to become sensitively aware of." Honoring another person means becoming sensitively aware of that person's essence (or spirit).

When I (Margot) want to relate to a small child who doesn't know me, I don't touch the child. I'll stop a short distance away. Then I'll send a loving vibration to surround them. I'll touch them, but not physically. Because they're so small, they might feel helpless and scared. So it's like touching them energetically.

Honoring is touching energetically, touching with the heart. The heart touches first before the body does.

TIP: CONNECT EARTH AND SPIRIT

This skill, called "The Heart Salutation" in *The Art of Sexual Ecstasy,* symbolizes bringing the energy of the earth to your heart and connecting your heart to your spirit. As your forehead touches your partner's forehead, you symbolically connect your spirit to your partner's spirit.

Homeplay

- Share this way of honoring another person—sitting or standing—with at least two other important people in your life. Ask them to describe their experience.

For additional ideas, read pages 56–62 of *The Art of Sexual Ecstasy.*

Give and Receive a Melting Hug

Benefits

- ༈ Experience a delicious whole-body, wholehearted connection
- ༈ Experience melting and surrendering

Purpose

- ༈ To feel that you are really present for each other
- ༈ To generate safety before you begin a Tantric practice
- ༈ To express your emotional support

Summary

You will need a partner, which could be a friend, lover, husband/wife, or even a child.

For two minutes, experiment giving each other a variety of different hugs. Play with them. Exaggerate them.

Then gently separate. Notice if you contracted or felt uncomfortable. Notice how the different hugs felt.

Now, shake off the ordinary hug experience. Standing a few steps apart, facing each other, begin with a standing Heart Salutation, honor your partner.

Pull the energy from the earth up to your heart on the inhale. On the exhale, bend forward at the waist, allowing foreheads to touch. On the next inhale, straighten your back. On the exhale, drop the hands and send energy back to the earth.

Now, slowly, very slowly, walk toward each other, maintaining eye contact and remaining as relaxed as possible. Allow your breathing to be deep and full, yet effortless. When you come near each other, open your arms in a welcoming gesture, with the palms of your hands open to each other.

Slowly touching, nestle against each other's chests, and wrap your arms gently around each other.

Allow your knees to drop and bend slightly. Relax your pelvis and move forward, touching the pelvis of your partner. Allow your knees to drop and touch your partner's knees. Allow your thighs and your bellies to connect.

Let your bodies relax here for a little while so that you melt into each other, giving yourselves over to a trusting embrace.

After a minute or two, notice your partner's breathing pattern. Let your own breathing harmonize with your partner's so that you softly inhale and exhale together. There is no place to go, nothing to do except relax.

No need to make any effort. Let go. This is about welcoming, receiving, surrendering, enjoying, melting, and dissolving into each other. That's why we call it the Melting Hug.

A Melting Hug can go on for a long time, until both people feel complete.

Take a few moments and share your experiences with each other.

(Modified from pages 78–82 of *The Art of Sexual Ecstasy.*)

SkyDancing Attitudes

- ⚘ Generate safety
- ⚘ Surrender and melt

Quick Steps

1. Give each other ordinary hugs. Notice.
2. Breathe deep. Welcome your partner.
3. Connect body parts. Nest chests. Drop knees. Touch pelvis. Touch knees, thighs, bellies.
4. Relax and melt into each other.

Your Experience

Describe your experience.

_____

_____

_____

_____

_____

_____

_____

TIP: AVOID THE NEEDY HUG

Melting does not mean *clinging* or *grabbing* or becoming *needy*. Avoid giving this impression. Avoid grabbing the other's body too tightly. Notice when you become needy, and then come back to your center.

Homeplay

- Teach the Melting Hug to at least three friends.
- Share at least one Melting Hug a day with your partner.

For additional ideas, read pages 78–82 of *The Art of Sexual Ecstasy*.

Open to Trust

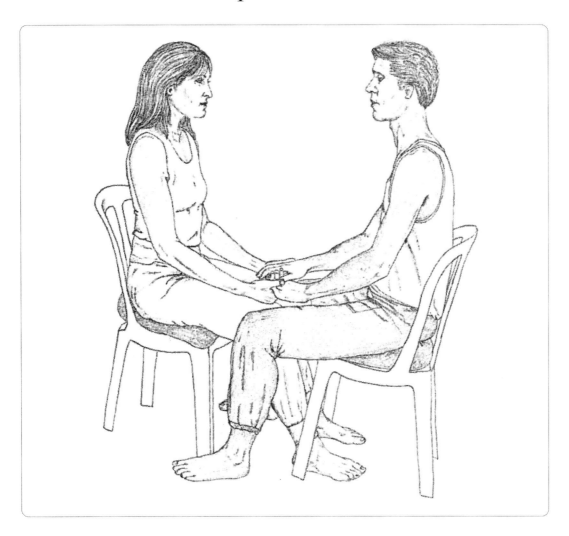

Benefits

- ☞ To develop your communication skills
- ☞ To be heard unconditionally
- ☞ To build intimacy and trust through honesty

Purpose

- ☞ To overcome shyness around sexual communication
- ☞ To communicate sexual fears and express your needs without shame
- ☞ To develop your ability to be fully present with your partner

Summary

Begin by honoring your partner with a Heart Salutation and Melting Hug. If you are single, we recommend that you find a friend to practice this skill with. If you are uncomfortable with a friend, we invite you to move beyond your discomfort. If you do this on your own, write down your own answers to the questions.

Sit comfortably facing your partner.

Each partner will have a chance to ask and answer each question. Allow your partner five to seven minutes to answer each question. Choose who will be the first speaker and who will be the first listener.

As the listener, give your partner your full attention. Stay centered and calm by breathing deeply. Remain a neutral observer, silent and sympathetic. When your partner finishes, be supportive. You may ask, "Is there anything else?"

Listener, ask the speaker the following questions.

Question #1: What are you most afraid of in your sex life?

First, define the fear in one or two sentences. For example, "I am afraid to pleasure myself in front of you." Always speak in the "I" mode; for example, "I am afraid _____."

Second, give a brief description of the last situation in which you felt this fear.

Listener, the healing step is for you to give your partner your full attention and presence. Be a neutral observer and breathe deeply. Avoid becoming personally involved right now. If you feel criticized, and you might well be, notice the urge to defend but stay silent; focus instead on your breath. Remember, this is your partner's process, not yours.

Listener, if your partner stops speaking, ask, "Is there anything else you would like to add?"

When your partner is finished, thank your partner by saying, "I appreciate you for sharing your fears."

Switch roles. End with a Heart Salutation.

Question #2: How would you like to be loved?

You want to teach your partner what works for you and how you want to be loved. In this way, you will be sure that when you are touched, your partner will know how to turn you on. In essence, you are giving them the first chapter of your own personal *Sexual Ecstasy User's Manual*.

So, say and show your partner the way to caress your face, head, lips, and breasts. For example, do you like your breasts kneaded like a baker kneads bread? Or, do you like your nipples to be rolled between the index finger and thumb? What kind of pressure and speed do you like? Be as specific and detailed as possible.

This may sound silly, yet often people don't ask for what they want in sex. Don't expect your partner to be a mind reader. Tell him or her what turns you on.

Talk about every part of your body, from the top of your head to the bottoms of your feet, including and especially your genitals.

How do you like your belly touched? Your arms? Your back? Your legs?

Be specific about how you want your penis, or your clitoris, caressed. Also, share what does not work for you.

Explain where your erogenous points are, such as inside the elbow, behind the ears, at the base of the spine, and so on.

When you've finished, both of you close your eyes for a moment to integrate the information. The one who was listening, ask yourself, "Did I really learn what I needed to learn in order for me to feel that I can love this person well?"

Speaker, ask yourself, "Did I really give enough information to teach my partner how to love me well?"

Then, open your eyes and appreciate each other.

Switch roles.

(Modified from pages 82–91 of *The Art of Sexual Ecstasy.*)

SkyDancing Attitudes

- ❧ Generate safety
- ❧ Celebrate sexuality and cultivate pleasure

Quick Steps

1. Sit comfortably facing your partner.
2. Ask (or answer) two questions:
   - What are your greatest sexual fears? Define the fear in one or two sentences: "I am afraid _____." Give a brief description of the last situation in which you felt this fear.
   - How would you like to be loved?
3. Ask, "Is there anything else?"
4. Switch roles.

Your Experience

Describe your experience. What did you find out about yourself that you didn't know? Where were you the most uncomfortable? What did you like about this activity?

_____

_____

_____

_____

_____

_____

_____

_____

_____

Tip: Check the Results

Describing how you want to be loved is a powerful skill. Equally important is listening to your partner and demonstrating in practice that you've heard what your partner said.

Soon after doing this practice, in your lovemaking you will know how well your partner listened to you.

If your partner really heard what you said and loves you enough to approximate what you asked for, it is much easier for you to really trust your partner and surrender more deeply.

On the other side, it is similar for your partner. Does your partner feel that you heard, that you're giving what your partner asked for, and that you're capable of staying centered while giving?

Do you enjoy what you are doing?

This little exercise is a wonderful way to get to know each other better and to open to trust.

Homeplay

- Make a date with your partner to share and heal more fears.
- Show your partner the second chapter of your own personal *Sexual Ecstasy User's Manual*.
- Describe your best sexual experience with each other and what made it special.
- Exercise your sexual communication muscles. Refine and describe in more detail how you like to be loved.

When you share what's going on in your mind, there is less need for mind-reading. The result is greater intimacy.

For additional ideas, read pages 82–91 of *The Art of Sexual Ecstasy*.

Stretch into Love

Benefits

- ⚘ Relax your body and release tension
- ⚘ Open more flow of energy through your body
- ⚘ Learn to dance between leading (yang) and following (yin)
- ⚘ Experience a state of relaxed alertness

Purpose

- ⚘ To open your body to experience more subtle sensations and erotic vibrations
- ⚘ To develop a dialogue between your two bodies as you learn how to trust, take the lead and follow, let go, and find a common rhythm
- ⚘ To prepare your body to be able to change positions easily during lovemaking

Summary

At the beginning of each SkyDancing Tantra practice, it is helpful to stretch your bodies. Doing so together will make stretching fun and playful.

If you are single, you can stretch by yourself. However, it is recommended that you find a friend to practice with. These practices can be done fully clothed, if you choose.

During the following stretches, it's important that you move at your own pace, be gentle with yourself and your partner. Practice deep breathing. Communicate any concerns or discomforts. If you experience tension in your body, relax and breathe into the area.

Here are two couples' stretches: "square stretch" and "slipping and sliding." Beyond these two, we invite you to experiment with creative ways in which both people can feel a stretch at the same time.

Notice how your interaction with your partner proceeds. Observe when and how you take the lead and when you give in and follow. Use the practice as a way of exploring the patterns in your relationship, seeing where you resist and where you respond and let go.

Gradually try loosening up your joints more while staying within the limits of what is comfortable.

When you're finished with a stretch, take a few moments to notice the changes in your body. Notice where you feel open and less tight.

Square Stretch

Sit, facing each other, legs outstretched, soles of feet against your partner's feet (or ankles, if one of you is considerably taller than the other, or has limited flexibility). Lean forward from the waist, keeping your spine as straight as possible. Firmly hold each other's wrists. Look into each other's eyes, and take some deep breaths.

Begin to sway gently backward and forward. Inhale through your mouth as you go backward, and exhale through your mouth as you come forward. Imagine that your breath is carrying the movement.

Test the range of your movements back and forth, and notice that the deeper you breathe, the wider your movements can go. Eventually, if your joints are relaxed enough, you may even be able to lie down with your back on the floor as you are inhaling and to bend forward with your forehead touching the ground between your partner's thighs as you're exhaling.

Keep your arms outstretched at all times.

Then, shift to moving in circles from the waist, clockwise and then counterclockwise. This movement easily becomes a rhythmic body dance. It is an excellent preparation for the bodily interplay of SkyDancing Tantra.

Feel how the hip joints, knee joints, and lower back loosen. This helps relax the pelvis during lovemaking. The loosening and centering is integral to releasing your sexual potential.

When you are finished, relax. When you're ready, talk for a few minutes about what you felt.

(Modified from pages 146–148 of *The Art of Sexual Ecstasy*.)

(See the DVD/video *The Art of Sexual Ecstasy,* listed in Resources.)

SLIPPING AND SLIDING

Because this practice will require you to cover each other with a lot of oil, you will want to protect your floor or bed with thick towels.

Remove your clothes.

Take some oil and lightly massage your partner all over with your hands and forearms.

Then use your outstretched body to massage and stretch your partner's back, pelvis, and legs. This teaches you to trust each other's body weight, which in turn helps you to explore different lovemaking positions more easily.

One partner should lie down while the other slides over him or her. Let the various parts of your two bodies slip sensuously over each other. Use your hands, feet, face, arms, legs, genitals, buttocks, and back. For example, bracing yourself with your arms, you can slide your breasts or genitals very slowly over your partner's entire body, starting at the feet and going right up the legs, pelvis, and chest, and across the face.

Keep your breathing deep, your body relaxed, and the atmosphere playful. Let your weight connect you with your partner; use your hands to keep from pressing down too much.

If you are receiving, generate safety by communicating when you are uncomfortable. Giver, check in with your partner periodically to see how he or she is doing.

When you are finished, relax. When you are ready, talk for a few minutes about what you felt. (Modified from pages 144–146 of *The Art of Sexual Ecstasy.*)

SkyDancing Attitudes

- ⚘ Generate safety
- ⚘ Celebrate sexuality and cultivate pleasure
- ⚘ Be childlike
- ⚘ Surrender and melt

Quick Steps

1. Move at your own pace. Breathe through tensions.
2. Try the "square stretch" and "slipping and sliding." Explore ways in which both partners can stretch at the same time.

3. Relax.

4. Talk for a few minutes about what you felt.

Your Experience

Describe your experience and what you felt.

_____

_____

_____

_____

_____

_____

_____

_____

_____

TIP: APPLY THREE KEYS TO ORGASMIC POWER

Remember to apply the three keys to orgasmic power: breathe, move, and make sounds—see "Dance the Three Keys to Orgasmic Power." (See p. 69.)

TIP: DEMONSTRATION AND MUSIC SELECTION

Use the DVD/video *The Art of Sexual Ecstasy* from Margot Anand, the CD *Music for Everyday Ecstasy*, the music CD *Stretch into Love* by Shastro, and the demonstration DVD from Philip Duane Johncock for additional tips and activities (see Resources).

Homeplay

⚘ Integrate stretching into your Tantric practices and lovemaking. Write down the new positions you have found where both partners feel a stretch at the same time and are also fun to do.

_____

_____

_____

_____

_____

_____

_____

_____

_____

_____

For additional ideas, read pages 144–162 of *The Art of Sexual Ecstasy.*

Breathe to Connect

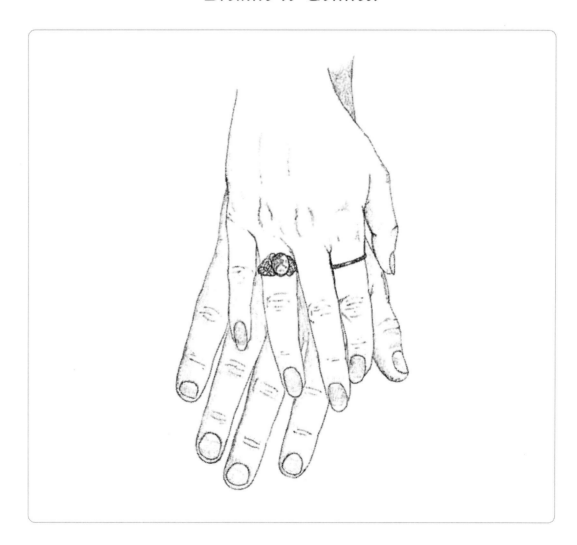

52

Benefit

- Bring awareness to your breathing and your touch
- Experience a deep, bonding relaxation with a partner

Purpose

- To notice how you connect energetically with your partner
- To learn how to use your breath to connect and bond with your partner

Summary

If you are single, find a friend with whom to do this practice.

You may do this practice fully clothed, if you wish.

For the first part of this activity, let your hand rest on your partner's hand. Notice any feelings and sensations this simple action brings up for you.

Then, notice your breath. Follow the feelings of the touch with your breath so that you become aware of how energy and consciousness interact.

Bring your breath and your awareness to your touch. Feel the energy that follows the action of touching. Give yourself a few minutes to breathe deeply and notice the flow of energy between your hand and your partner's.

The second step of the process is to lie next to your partner, in a spoon position. Relax your body completely and melt into your partner.

Notice your breathing. Is it relaxed? How is your partner's breathing rhythm? Is it slower or faster than yours? Can you adjust your rhythms together?

Allow the rhythm of your breath to match your partner's breathing rhythm. Relax until both breaths become one breath, one pulse. Take your time. Luxuriate in melting into each other's breath.

Let any unexpressed feelings, such as resentments and worries, be fully released as you ex-

Spoon Position

hale. Feel yourself becoming lighter each time you exhale. It's a beautiful feeling to allow yourself so much trust that you can simply lie there and let the other person in.

The more sensitive and transparent you become, the more you begin to feel formless. Give expression to your softness and vulnerability. You can let go. You generate safety. You are welcoming each other more and more as you relax.

When you're finished, share with each other your experiences.

(Modified from pages 50–55 and 290–295 of *The Art of Sexual Ecstasy.*)

SkyDancing Attitudes

- Generate safety
- View sexuality as energy
- Surrender and melt

Quick Steps

1. Rest your hand on your partner's hand. Notice feelings. Breathe into your feelings. Notice what happens.
2. Lie in the spoon position. Watch your breathing and your partner's breathing. Relax your body completely. Melt into your partner.
3. Allow your breathing rhythms to become one.
4. Share your experiences.

Your Experience

Describe your experience.

_____

_____

_____

_____

_____

_____

_____

_____

_____

_____

_____

Tip: Watch the Breath

Watch the movement of your breath rather than paying attention to your thoughts.

Tip: Apply to Lovemaking or Just Relaxing

You can apply this principle of connecting energy and consciousness through the breath in any love position or when just relaxing in each other's arms.

Tip: Change Positions

Readjust your position or tell each other if you need to move during this exploration. Remember, any movement has to be slow, deliberate, and gentle.

Tip: Let Go of Quick Ecstasy Expectation

Avoid the trap of expecting cosmic ecstasy after five minutes. Cultivate pleasure. You may feel disappointed if nothing special happens at first. Each new step needs to be repeated several times before you get the hang of it.

Homeplay

- Extend this practice to include looking into each other's eyes and breathing together.
- Add the scissors position (see illustration).
- When you have explored relaxing together in the spooning, scissors, or other positions, take it a step further. Apply it to your lovemaking.

Scissors Position

For additional ideas, read pages 50–55 and 290–295 of
The Art of Sexual Ecstasy.

Expand Sexual Pleasure

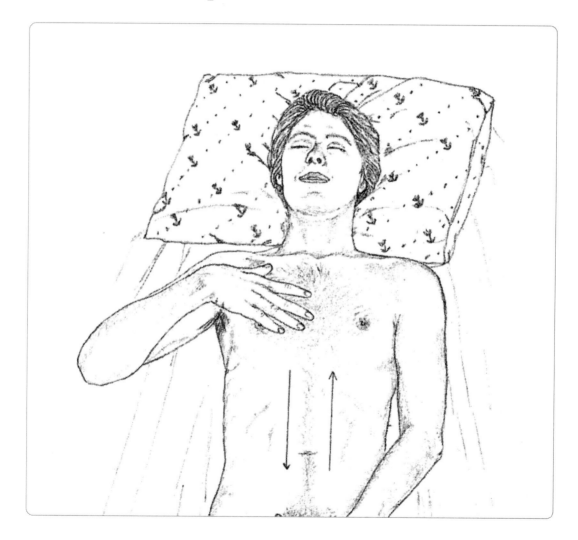

Benefits

- ❧ Women: heighten your sexual pleasure considerably; learn how to achieve a whole-body orgasm independently of sexual penetration
- ❧ Men: acquire greater staying power and a stronger erection, as well as ability to spread pleasurable sensations beyond the genitals

Purpose

- ❧ To increase the buildup of sexual arousal and then spread sexual energy to other parts of the body

Summary

This skill can be practiced alone or with a partner.

You may wish to record this summary on a tape or CD to listen to as you practice this skill. Or you may guide your partner.

Soft, sensual music in the background will enhance the experience. Select your favorite music or use the music CD specially composed for this skill, called *Sexual Breathing*. (See Resources for more information.)

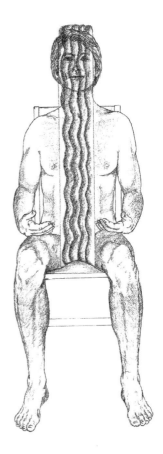

VISUALIZE INNER FLUTE

Stand or sit toward the front of a hard-backed chair or lie comfortably on the floor on your back. Begin by visualizing an inner channel running from the top of your head to the perineum point (perineal muscles) midway between your genitals and anus. In acupuncture, this if often called the "middle meridian." Traditionally, the Taoists have called this secret channel the Hollow

Bamboo. We call it the Inner Flute, because we experience it as an instrument on which we can teach ourselves and others to play the most ecstatic music. That is, you can use the Inner Flute to circulate orgasmic energy through the whole body.

PC Pump

Next, lie on your back. Begin to tighten and relax the pubococcygeus (PC) muscle in quick, short pulsations. The PC muscle spreads out like butterfly wings at the bottom of the pelvis to connect the anus and genitals to the sitting bones and legs. The PC muscle lies exactly between the genitals and anus, so focus your awareness in this area. Make short, quick pulses with the PC muscle until you have a good feeling for it.

Now bring in your breathing. Inhale, contracting the PC muscle as you do so, keeping the rest of your body relaxed, especially your shoulders. As you exhale, relax the PC muscle. Do not hold your breath on the inhale or exhale.

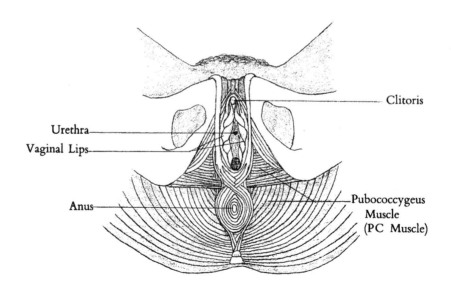

Next, squeeze and pump the PC muscle as you inhale. Then, hold your breath for a count of six seconds. Imagine that you want to urinate and are trying to hold in a full bladder.

Exhale, relaxing the PC muscle.

Inhale and pump the PC muscle, hold, exhale, and relax. Do this for five minutes. We call this the PC Pump.

SEXUAL BREATHING COMBINED WITH PC PUMP

Now add in Sexual Breathing. Again, you can do this standing, sitting, or lying down. Let your left hand rest gently on your genitals. Let your right hand cover your left hand. Feel that you are cradling and protecting your genitals. Close your eyes.

When you're ready, feeling relaxed and energized, combine Sexual Breathing with the PC Pump. Inhale, contract the PC muscle, and imagine that your breath is entering through your genitals. Exhale, relax the PC muscle. and imagine the air flowing out through your genitals. Do this a few times.

SEXUAL BREATHING THROUGH THE INNER FLUTE

Now inhale, contract the PC muscle, and imagine that you are sucking in air through your genitals; slowly move your right hand up your body toward your heart and forehead as you in-

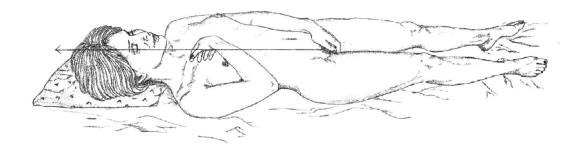

hale. When you reach your forehead, pause and hold your breath for a few seconds. Then, as you exhale, move your hand down your body back to your genitals. In effect, you are tracing the flow of air as it moves up and down your Inner Flute.

Inhale, squeeze the PC muscle, and imagine you are pulling the breath with the sexual energy up to your forehead. Exhale, relax the PC muscle, and imagine your breath and sexual energy trickling down slowly from your forehead, to your heart, belly, and into your genitals. Do this for a few minutes.

PELVIC ROCKING

Finally, add a rocking movement of your pelvis. This is a slower, more deliberate version of the spontaneous movement of the body's reflex during orgasm.

Lift your knees up till you can place the soles of your feet on the floor. Play with rocking your pelvis back, arching your back off the floor on the inhale, allowing your belly to get big. Exhale and flatten your back. Inhale, arch your back, tailbone pointed down into the floor. Exhale, relax your belly, flatten your back, and melt into the floor.

COMBINE ALL STEPS

Now you're ready to combine all parts. On the next inhale, squeeze the PC muscle, pull sexual energy up to your forehead, and arch your back. Exhale, flatten your back, and relax the PC muscle. Allow the energy to drop down and be pushed out through your genitals.

A gentle pace will do, a four-second count. Inhale . . . pump the PC muscle, pull sexual energy up to your forehead, rock your pelvis back, arch your back—one . . . two . . . three . . . four. Exhale, relax the PC muscle, allow energy to drop down, flatten your back, push the energy down and out your genitals—one . . . two . . . three . . . four.

Do this for a few minutes, remembering to relax your pelvis and jaw.

Finish by spooning or cuddling for a few minutes. Relax alone or with your partner. Notice the energy vibrating through your body.

(Modified from pages 163–188 of *The Art of Sexual Ecstasy*.)

SkyDancing Attitudes

- ❧ Celebrate sexuality and cultivate pleasure
- ❧ View sexuality as energy
- ❧ Connect sex with heart and spirit

Quick Steps

1. Visualize Inner Flute.
2. Pulse and pump the PC muscle on inhale. Exhale, relax.
3. Pull sexual energy from genitals to forehead on inhale, and then back to genitals on exhale.
4. Rock pelvis back, arch back, let belly rise on inhale. Exhale, flatten back, relax belly, push energy down and out though the genitals. Melt into the floor.
5. Combine all four steps.
6. Relax. Spoon or cuddle.
7. Share your experience.

Your Experience

Describe your experience.

_____

_____

_____

_____

_____

_____

_____

_____

Tip: Different Positions

This skill can be practiced in many different positions (alone, lying down, sitting, facing your partner, while making love, during self-pleasuring).

Tip: Advanced Pelvic Rocking

On Pelvic Rocking with a partner, see "Harmonize with the Heart Wave" (page 76).

Tip: Film Demonstration

For a complete demonstration on how to expand sexual pleasure, including Sexual Breathing and Pelvic Rocking, watch the DVD/video *The Art of Sexual Pleasure* (see Resources).

Homeplay

- Practice pumping your PC muscle at red lights, during business meetings, and especially if you have to sit for long periods of time.
- Practice sexual breathing to expand sexual pleasure during self-pleasuring.
- Try Pelvic Rocking and breathing to expand sexual pleasure while sitting up and facing your partner.

For additional ideas, read pages 163–192 of *The Art of Sexual Ecstasy.*

Give a Voice to Your Sexual Organs

Benefits

- ✎ Understand and express your sexual needs better
- ✎ Experience humor and laughter in the context of sexual communication

Purpose

- ✎ To express your sexual moods and needs without emotional charge

Summary

Sit in front of your partner. One partner speaks, while the other just listens and remains silent. If you are single, sit in front of a mirror. You can be either dressed or naked, depending on how advanced you want to make it.

If you are doing this with a partner, close your eyes and put your hands on your genitals. Give your sexual organs a name. You may have a pet name that you like or imagine a new one. In SkyDancing trainings, "Yoni" ("cosmic womb" in Sanskrit) is the name given to the female genitals, and "Vajra" ("thunderbolt" in Sanskrit) is the name given to the penis.

Allow your sexual organs to speak to you, to tell you the name they would like to be called, right now, for this practice.

Now give your genitals a voice. For instance: "I am happy to live with Margot," or "I'm happy or unhappy she keeps me under the table and she keeps writing books." They may say, "I'm rusty and out of practice," or "It's about time you gave me some attention."

Let [the name you give your genitals] talk and say whatever he or she wants to say.

Let him or her talk about the current state of affairs. How does he or she feel living with you? What can you do to be in harmony with your sexual center (yoni or vajra)? Do you listen to the needs of that part of yourself?

Play with giving voice to your sexual organs. Let them speak for as long as needed.

Now switch roles.

SkyDancing Attitudes

- Be childlike
- Celebrate sexuality and cultivate pleasure
- Connect sex with heart and spirit

Quick Steps

1. Sit in front of your partner or a mirror.
2. Close your eyes and put your hands on your genitals.
3. Give your sexual organs a name.
4. Let [the name you give your genitals] speak. Give him or her a voice and authentic expression.
5. Switch roles.

Your Experience

Describe your experience.

_____

_____

_____

_____

_____

_____

_____

_____

TIP: EXPRESS DELICATE THINGS WITH FUN

This sexual dialogue is very useful when you want to find a fun way to express delicate things around sexual needs. For example, instead of saying, "I am aroused and I want to make love," you might say, "Cherry Blossom [your vagina's name] feels very perky and is asking for some action. She wants a visit."

Homeplay

- Give voice to your sexual organs at least once a week for the next five weeks.
- Write what your genitals say in your journal, or share it with your partner or a friend.

Dance the Three Keys to Orgasmic Power

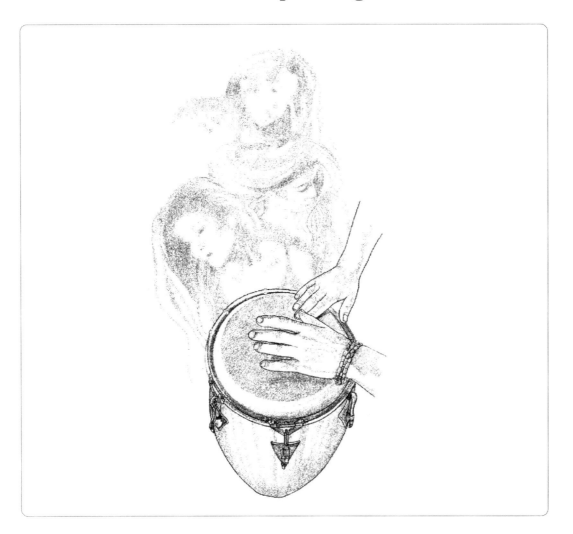

Benefits

- 🌱 To shake loose stress and tension
- 🌱 To play with the voluntary and involuntary orgasmic responses
- 🌱 To enhance orgasmic pleasure

Purpose

- 🌱 To open your body to experience whole-body orgasms
- 🌱 To apply the three keys to orgasmic power to build up and discharge sexual energy

Summary

You can do this alone or with a partner or even with a group.

To warm up, take a few minutes to stand and rub the palms of your hands together. Then, massage your face and rub your hands over your body. It is helpful to play some fast-paced music for this activity.

Next, shake loose all the joints in your body. Start with your toes and go up your body—feet, knees, pelvis, spine, shoulders, elbows, wrists, fingers, neck, jaw, and head. Spend a few minutes playing with how you can creatively shake loose all the joints in your body. Shake off all the stress and tension in your body.

For the next ten to fifteen minutes, play with unrestricted, unconditional dancing. No conditions, no restrictions.

Play with deep breathing, whole-body movement and making sounds, the three keys to your orgasmic power.

Focus on deep breathing through your mouth. Relax your jaw. Move every part of your body as you breathe into that part.

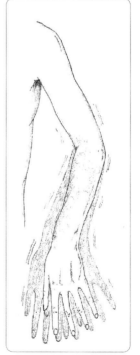

If you lift an arm, inhale while you do it. If you shake a leg, exhale into your leg while you shake it. Play with breathing deeply and noticing what happens to your body. Go all the way with your breathing.

Feel how deep breathing expands your body's movement. Allow the breath to carry the body's movement. As you dance or move, feel as if your breath carries each movement.

Move from the inside. When you lift an arm, imagine the arm is lifted by your inhale.

Then, explore dancing emotions. Get in touch with something you feel sad about. Dance your sadness for a minute.

Get in touch with something you feel angry about. Allow your movement to match your anger. Dance your anger with your arms and legs. Make growling sounds. Dance and vocalize your anger for a minute.

Notice something you feel afraid about. Let your fear dance. Give it shape. Dance your fear for a minute.

Get in touch with something you are happy about. Dance and vocalize your joy. Dance your joy for a minute.

Notice any sexual sensations in your body. Let your sexual energy dance. Dance and vocalize your sexual energy for a minute.

Feel how the breath can amplify your movements and the sensations in your body. This is what happens during sexual orgasm.

Now, using your voice, make sounds that give a "color" and "feel" to your energy. Express the sensations in your body with your voice—giggle, scream, jump.

Let your emotions out. Give sound to your sadness, anger, fear, joy, and sexual feelings. Use your breath to amplify your movements and sounds.

Allow yourself to go crazy, look silly. Make faces with your sounds. Play with your tongue and vocal chords in new and fun ways. Try "gibberish": sounds without meaning that "tell a story."

Make sounds for five to ten minutes.

Gradually begin to slow your breath, movement, and sounds. Close your eyes and bring the energy you are experiencing inside, contain your energy. Allow the vibrations of energy to ripple through your body.

THE BUTTERFLY

If you are doing this with a partner, allow yourself to come into the butterfly position. The person who feels most yang (supportive) sits with spread legs, while the yin (needing support)

person lies on his or her back with his or her head between the partner's legs. Hold on to your partner's hands; while your arms stay relaxed, look into each other's eyes.

If you are doing this alone, lie down and relax. You may want to curl up with a pillow or teddy bear.

As you relax, notice the energy sensations rippling through your body. Allow the energy to expand throughout your whole body, your whole being.

SkyDancing Attitudes

- Celebrate sexuality and cultivate pleasure
- View sexuality as energy
- Love your inner rebel

Quick Steps

1. Shake loose. Shake your joints.
2. Breathe deeply through your mouth. Relax your jaw. Breathe into and out of various parts of your body.
3. Move your body parts voluntarily and involuntarily. Move from inside. Dance your feelings: sadness, anger, fear, joy, and sexual feelings.
4. Throw out as many different sounds as you can.
5. End in the butterfly position. Relax.
6. Notice the energy streams running through your body.

Your Experience

Describe your experience.

_____

_____

_____

_____

_____

_____

_____

_____

TIP: BREATHE

Breathe deeply through your mouth. Relax your jaw. Deep breathing speeds up the body's metabolism, increases energy charge, and speeds up energy discharge. Your energy level rises, and the nerve endings beneath your skin become more sensitive, resulting in a sense of tingling and vibrancy.

TIP: MOVE

Allow sensations, feelings, and the breath to move your body and expand. It is much harder to get energy streaming through your body when you are motionless than it is when your body moves, dances, undulates.

Let your body act out what is going on inside. Become the dance. Even small movements expand sensations in your body.

> ## TIP: MAKE SOUNDS
>
> Ecstasy comes only when we let our feelings loose. Give voice to your pleasure, as well as the blocks. Use sighs, shouts, animal sounds, gibberish, crying, however the spirit moves you. Don't censor your expression or hold back. Go for it!
>
> Sounds give color and tone to your energy, increase your sense of release, and help your partner to know what you're feeling.
>
> ## TIP: MUSIC SELECTION
>
> Use *Dance the Three Keys to Orgasmic Power* music and guided activity CDs by Margot Anand and Philip Duane Johncock (see Resources for more information).

Homeplay

- Dance the three keys of your orgasmic power at least once a week.
- Find new music that invokes breath, movement, and sound in you.
- Use Margot Anand's *Sexual Breathing* CD (see Resources).
- Find new ways to breathe, move, and vocalize in all that you do.
- Experiment with bringing breath, movement, and sound into your self-pleasuring and lovemaking.

For additional ideas, read pages 130–131 and 271–299 of
The Art of Sexual Ecstasy.

Harmonize with the Heart Wave

Benefits

- Build up an energetic connection between sex and heart in yourself and with your partner
- Allow yourself to explore being receptive (yin), letting the other lead, and then switching to taking the lead yourself (yang)
- Release, in a joyful manner, pent-up energies, such as unexpressed frustrations
- Deepen your practice and application of the three keys to orgasmic power: deep breathing, movement, and voice
- Create love and harmony in your relationship

Purpose

- To gently fine-tune each other's rhythm through movement, breathing, making sounds, and playing
- To practice the three keys to orgasmic power in a relationship context

Summary

The Heart Wave is a partner practice. You can practice this skill fully clothed if you choose.

Sit comfortably on a pillow or cushion. When you sit opposite your partner, begin by honoring your partner with a Heart Salutation. Close your eyes. Draw your attention and breath to your sex center. Breathe all the way to your navel, your gravity center.

Hand Dance

Raise your arms together. Allow the tip of your fingers to connect with the tip of your partner's fingers. Breathing through the mouth, from your belly, breathe deeply. Begin to sway your arms, pressing against each other's hands.

Let yourself be guided by your partner. Or guide your partner. Play with being yin (receptive) and yang (active). Enter into a playful hand dance until you reach an equilibrium where neither of you is guiding or being guided.

Let your inner rebel out and play by saying "nah-nah-nah-nah-nah" and pushing with your hands.

Imagine you are dancing an animal mating ritual. First, aggressively make loud noises. Then seductively make cooing sounds.

After five minutes or so of playing, slow down, bring your arms down, bring your attention inside, rest.

OPEN THE INNER FLUTE

This is a new application of the Pelvic Rocking practice introduced in "Expand Sexual Pleasure" (see page 58). Here you will use Pelvis Rocking with a partner.

Slowly begin to move your pelvis back and forth in unison with your slow breathing. Imagine your pelvis is like a round ball, rolling on itself.

After a few minutes of rocking, add the PC Pump, contracting and relaxing the muscles around your anus and genitals.

Once you feel a warm or tingling sensation in your pelvis, visualize your breath traveling up the Inner Flute to your heart center and back down to your sex as you continue to rock your pelvis back and forth together with pumping the PC muscle. Keep your body as relaxed as possible. Continue for five minutes.

Now add Sexual Breathing. Draw the movement of your breath with your hand. Imagine energy entering through your sex as you inhale from your sex to your heart and exhale it back to your sex. Do this for a few breaths.

HEART WAVE

Now inhale through your sex to your heart. On the exhale, visualize energy and light going from your heart into your partner's heart and down through his or her Inner Flute, from the heart to the sex. Inhale energy from your partner's sex into your sex, then to your heart. Create a cycle of energy between your sex and heart to your partner's heart and sex, and back to you.

At the same time, your partner does the same breath and visualization.

The Sexual Breathing remains gentle and flowing without holding between inhale and exhale. Allow your mind to be completely transparent and raise your awareness to the merging of energies, the connection between the two of you. Continue for approximately five minutes.

RIDE THE WAVE OF BLISS

If you're with a partner and comfortable, move into the Wave of Bliss position (the woman on the man's lap). Connect your hearts. Join your breathing. Embrace as long as you wish.

Wave of Bliss

End by honoring your partner with a Heart Salutation.

Share your experiences with each other.

(Modified from pages 403–423 of *The Art of Sexual Ecstasy.*)

SkyDancing Attitudes

- Celebrate sexuality and cultivate pleasure
- Be childlike
- View sexuality as energy
- Connect sex with heart and spirit
- Love and express your inner rebel

Quick Steps

1. Sit comfortably on pillow or zafu (a Zen meditation pillow).
2. Connect and play with hands.
3. Begin Pelvic Rocking. Add pumping of the PC muscle and Sexual Breathing. Visualize energy coming up your Inner Flute.
4. Explore the Heart Wave, cycling energy from genitals to heart to your partner's heart and genitals, then back through your genitals.
5. Sit in Wave of Bliss position (one partner on the other's lap).
6. Share your experiences.

Your Experience

Describe your experience.

_____

_____

_____

_____

_____

TIP: TAKE IT EASY

You may want to practice each of the four steps of this skill separately. For example, practice the Hand Dance. Practice the Heart Wave later. That is fine. Go at your own pace.

TIP: WAVE OF BLISS

For more detailed guidance on the Wave of Bliss, see the DVD/video *The Art of Sexual Ecstasy* (see Resources).

TIP: FIND THE PEARL

Remember that you may need to practice these steps at least once a week for several months to really go deep and draw forth the pearls from this practice. Stay with it. You'll be glad you did. What you get will definitely be worth the time and effort!

Homeplay

- To integrate the Heart Wave into your lovemaking, the next time you make love, make love normally. Then switch to the Heart Wave for a few minutes (as long as it feels comfortable). Go back to lovemaking. Periodically switch to the Heart Wave until practicing with lovemaking becomes ecstatic. This does happen!

For additional ideas, read pages 403–423 of *The Art of Sexual Ecstasy.*

Awaken Your Senses

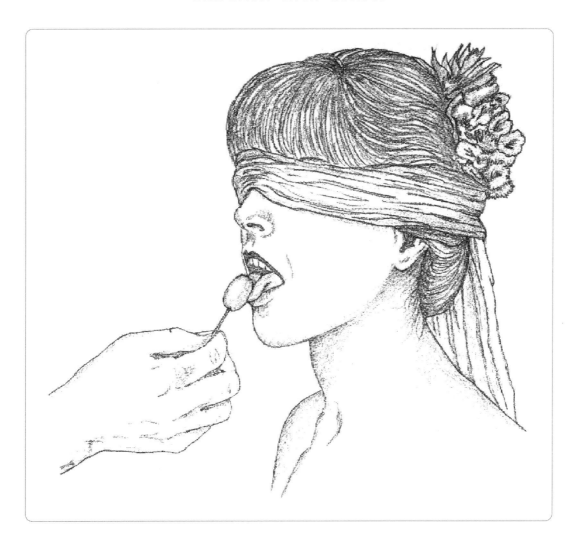

Benefits

- ❧ Play in the world of sensual delight
- ❧ Play with giving and receiving pleasure

Purpose

- ❧ To open the doors of perception and heighten sensory awareness
- ❧ To practice the arts of teasing and seduction
- ❧ To offer a creative gift of pleasure to your partner

Summary

You will need a partner for this practice. You can also practice this skill with a group of people, some givers and some receivers.

For this activity, you will need to prepare your safe space and some items ahead of time. Some helpful ideas:

- ❧ Hearing: shakers, bells, cymbals, bowls, drums, tambourines, musical instruments—whatever you can think of that will make beautiful and fun sounds; prepare soft background music for each sense. I (Philip) like to make a CD or tape with a compilation of music for each sense.
- ❧ Smell: flower essences, essential oils (such as peppermint, eucalyptus, ylang-ylang), orange peels, fragrant flowers—whatever you can think of that is aromatic
- ❧ Taste: sensuous food, such as seedless grapes, small chunks of pineapple, lychee nuts, strawberries, chocolates, your favorite liqueur—whatever you can think of that would awaken the taste buds
- ❧ Touch: feathers (soft ones, like peacock and ostrich feathers), silk fabric, a piece of fur—whatever you can think of that would feel great on the skin

🖋 Sight: prepare a beautiful environment, full of plants, flowers, colored scarves, artworks, soft candlelight, and other beautiful objects visually decorative.

Create a setting for your partner that is relaxing and comfortable. Have candles, soft music, and incense ready.

Blindfold your partner outside of the room so he or she cannot see anything upon entering the space. Then, take your partner on a short journey (blindfolded) with the destination being your safe space. Have the blindfolded partner sit on a chair or on pillows on the floor.

Give your partner the instructions that his or her only job is "to receive." Invite the blindfolded partner to "breathe deeply, relax, enjoy, and receive."

Now spend some time—say five minutes—with each sense, teasing and playing with your partner. Take your time with this ritual so the receiver can fully experience each item.

Go through each item, each sense, deliberately, slowly. You'll find that giving is an art form, one to enjoy deeply and gently.

Allow your partner to experience each item for each sense for one minute so as to integrate the experience before you go on to the next sense.

- Hearing: Switch to different sounds from different corners of the room. Play with coming closer and going farther away. Avoid getting too close to the ears.
- Smell: Invite your partner to inhale each smell deeply.
- Taste: Using a toothpick, dip the fruits or chocolates into liqueur. (If you don't drink alcohol, skip the liqueur.) Let your partner smell first. Then brush the item on their lips. Go away. Come back. Tease!
- Touch: Using a feather, caress and tickle your partner in unexpected places—earlobes, nipples, hollow of the hand—until he or she laughs.

Finish the touching segment by moving behind your partner, placing your hand on the heart center, supporting his or her body with yours. Allow the blindfolded partner to experience being supported and loved after this wonderful experience.

❧ Sight: Gently remove your partner's blindfold. Encourage him or her to look around at the beauty that surrounds you with "fresh eyes," as if for the first time, as a newborn.

Remember to allow your partner a minute of silence after each sense before moving on to the next sense.

You may choose to switch roles, or wait until another occasion to switch.

(Modified from pages 96–105 of *The Art of Sexual Ecstasy.*)

SkyDancing Attitudes

❧ Generate safety

❧ Celebrate sexuality and cultivate pleasure

❧ Surrender and melt

Quick Steps

1. Collect the items for smell, hearing, taste, and touch.
2. Blindfold partner. Tease and play with the items for each sense.
3. Move slowly and deliberately. Take your time. Enjoy your role as giver.
4. Go through each sense. Leave a minute of silence and stillness between each transition.
5. Play different music for each sense.
6. Switch roles.

Your Experience

Describe your experience.

_____

_____

_____

_____

_____

_____

_____

_____

_____

_____

_____

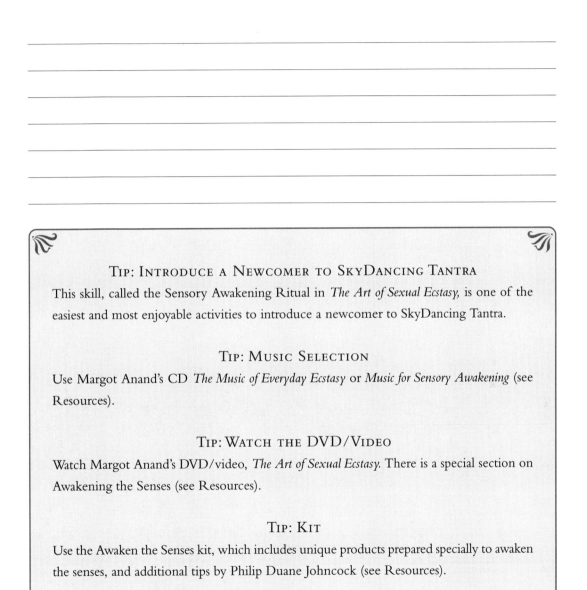

TIP: INTRODUCE A NEWCOMER TO SKYDANCING TANTRA

This skill, called the Sensory Awakening Ritual in *The Art of Sexual Ecstasy,* is one of the easiest and most enjoyable activities to introduce a newcomer to SkyDancing Tantra.

TIP: MUSIC SELECTION

Use Margot Anand's CD *The Music of Everyday Ecstasy* or *Music for Sensory Awakening* (see Resources).

TIP: WATCH THE DVD/VIDEO

Watch Margot Anand's DVD/video, *The Art of Sexual Ecstasy.* There is a special section on Awakening the Senses (see Resources).

TIP: KIT

Use the Awaken the Senses kit, which includes unique products prepared specially to awaken the senses, and additional tips by Philip Duane Johncock (see Resources).

Homeplay

- Give the Sensory Awakening Ritual as a gift to a friend.
- Give that special someone the Ritual as a gift for a birthday, special occasion, or just out of the kindness of your heart. First set a date. Don't let your friend know what is going to happen. Tell your friend to meet you at a specific time near the safe space you create (off-limits to your friend until the ceremony). Then lead your partner blindfolded around and into the safe space.
- Ask your partner to give you a Sensory Awakening Ritual surprise gift in return.

For additional ideas, read pages 96–105 of *The Art of Sexual Ecstasy.*

Play the Yin/Yang Game

Benefits

- ✻ Be continually surprised, while building trust and intimacy
- ✻ Experience asking for what you want in a fun, playful way
- ✻ Dare to feel you deserve the best

Purpose

- ✻ To harmonize the male and female aspects of your nature with each other
- ✻ To create clarity in your relationships
- ✻ To learn how to be a creative and generous lover

Summary

This game can be played between two partners—friends, lovers, husband and wife.

To start the game, each person goes alone to a quiet place with pen and paper. Write your response to "My day in heaven would be . . ." or "What I've always wanted to receive and never dared to ask for is . . ." Make a complete list of your wishes, even the most outrageous ones. Keep writing until nothing more comes to mind.

Then review the list and prioritize the items that are feasible, doable, on this day, for this game.

When you have finished, meet with your partner in a safe space you have created. Honor each other with a Heart Salutation. Then decide who is to start the game as the yang (active) partner and who is to be the yin (supportive) partner. Then read and discuss your lists with each other. Or you may choose not to tell each other anything in advance. Surprises are fun, too!

It is the yin partner's task to carry out the desires of the yang partner. After ten minutes, have one minute of silence. Then switch roles.

Keep playing and switching roles (ten minutes for playing, followed by one minute of silence).

Some sample requests might be: "I want to be five years old and cuddled for an hour. Hold me tight . . . and tell me you love me." Or, "When I wake up, I want you to serve me breakfast in bed." Or, "I want to lie down naked by the fireplace while you cover my body with flowers and dollar bills." Or, "Seduce me on the kitchen table."

(Modified from pages 257–270 of *The Art of Sexual Ecstasy*.)

SkyDancing Attitudes

- ⚘ Generate safety
- ⚘ Celebrate sexuality and cultivate pleasure
- ⚘ Be childlike
- ⚘ Surrender and melt
- ⚘ Love your inner rebel

Quick Steps

1. Write down your response to "My ideal day in heaven would be . . ." or "What I've always wanted to receive and never dared to ask for is . . ." Make your wish list.
2. Review list and prioritize doable items.
3. Play yin partner or yang partner for ten minutes each. Have a minute of silence before switching.
4. Switch roles.
5. Switch roles as often as you like.

Your Experience

Describe your experience as the yin partner (the supporter carrying out the desires of the yang partner).

_____

_____

_____

_____

_____

_____

_____

_____

_____

_____

_____

_____

Describe your experience as the yang partner (your desires are fulfilled by the yin partner).

_____

_____

_____

_____

_____

_____

_____

_____

_____

_____

_____

Tip: Suggestions for Yang Partner

Take full responsibility for making your desires and fantasies come true. You are a king (or queen). You have the right to ask for anything you wish, for the fulfillment of any fantasy. Be daring, inventive, and creative, beyond the ordinary limitations of everyday life. You are learning what you like, how you like it, and how much of it you want. You are learning how to receive more pleasure.

Avoid giving tasks to your yin partner that could be unpleasant or perceived as a punishment. Devise a scenario that will benefit both of you.

Be compassionate and generous. Develop the subtle skill of receptive awareness of yin. Ask for only as much as your supporter can assimilate at any given moment. Invent tasks that will be pleasing to you and also to your yin partner.

Tip: Suggestions for Yin Partner

As yin, you are the nurturing one who helps yang to realize his or her wishes. For this period, the other becomes more important than you. Think of the unconditional acceptance of a mother toward her young child.

As the yin partner, you are training in the art of moving from no to yes. Saying no gives a sense of being in control, of power. But naysaying can also degenerate into fear of exploring new, unknown, risky situations that confront our fixed attitudes toward life.

Saying yes opens you up to new challenges. You become willing to act without imposing your own likes and dislikes on your partner. In this way, you discover precious moments of feeling "egoless" and transparent.

Being yin does not mean, however, that you have to do whatever the other person asks. You are not a slave who should not question, be totally subservient, or lose face.

As yin, you are training in the art of truthful surrender to yang. This means saying yes in many different situations so that you can touch the feminine principle inside you at its deepest level.

If a request does not feel right, though, say, "Beloved, I feel unable to follow your request. Could you possibly change your wish so that I may support you within the limits of my capabilities?"

TIP: PLAY LONGER

You may choose to play the game for a longer period of time. For example, switch every hour or even every two or three hours. This will allow you to go deeper.

Homeplay

 For a change of pace, try doing the Yin/Yang Game (see page 91) for thirty to sixty minutes once every week. This will break up routines and bring in a deep level of play and creativity.

For additional ideas, read pages 257–270 of *The Art of Sexual Ecstasy.*

Appreciate

Benefits

- ⚘ Increase flow of positive energy
- ⚘ Learn the art of giving and receiving gifts of appreciation

Purpose

- ⚘ To create a positive flow of energy through appreciating of self and partner

Summary

This skill has two phases: self-appreciate and appreciate your partner.

Sit comfortably in front of your partner. Visualize that you have a treasure chest in front of the two of you. If you're on your own, you can write your appreciations on separate pieces of paper, fold them, and put them in an actual treasure chest. Then, revisit them in your daily appreciations of yourself.

If you do this with your partner, imagine that this treasure chest contains all the gifts that you have received from yourself and each other and that you want to give each other. They are also appreciations that you have noted as the most important discoveries you made through the practice of these skills.

SELF-APPRECIATE

Speaker, begin sharing out loud your appreciations for yourself. Visualize your appreciations being placed in the treasure chest in front of you: *"I appreciate myself for . . ."*

Listener, repeat what you hear the speaker say. *"I hear that you appreciate yourself for . . ."*

Speaker, share your appreciations for two to three minutes.

Switch roles.

New speaker, visualize your appreciations being placed in the treasure chest in front of you: *"I appreciate myself for . . ."*

New listener, repeat what you hear the speaker say: *"I hear that you appreciate yourself for . . ."*

Speaker, share your appreciations for two to three minutes.

Switch roles again.

APPRECIATE YOUR PARTNER

Original speaker, say out loud your appreciations for your partner. Visualize your appreciations being placed in the treasure chest in front of you: *"I appreciate you for . . ."*

Original listener, repeat what you hear the speaker say: *"I hear that you appreciate me for . . ."*

Speaker, share your appreciations for two to three minutes.

Switch roles.

New speaker, visualize your appreciations being placed in the treasure chest in front of you: *"I appreciate you for . . ."*

New listener, repeat what you hear the speaker say: *"I hear that you appreciate me for . . ."*

Speaker, share your appreciations for two to three minutes.

End the appreciation session by honoring each other with a Heart Salutation and a Melting Hug.

SkyDancing Attitudes

- ⚘ Celebrate sexuality and cultivate pleasure
- ⚘ Be childlike
- ⚘ View sexuality as energy

Quick Steps

1. Visualize a treasure chest between you and your partner.
2. Take turns sharing out loud: "I appreciate myself for . . ." and "I hear that you appreciate yourself for . . ."

3. Take turns sharing out loud: "I appreciate you for . . ." and "I hear that you appreciate me for . . ."

4. If you explore on your own, repeat the other steps for yourself alone or in partnership with your Inner Lover. Write down your appreciations.

Your Experience

Describe your experience giving and receiving appreciations.

_____

_____

_____

_____

_____

_____

_____

TIP: LETTING APPRECIATIONS LAND

Often it is a challenge for one to give appreciations to oneself or receive appreciations from one's partner. When you are being appreciated, notice how far into your body the appreciation lands energetically. Did it not even make it into your body? Did the appreciation make it down as far as your neck? Or did it make it all the way to your heart and even down to your toes? Open your body posture to be more receptive. Give yourself time to absorb the appreciation, to let it sink in. Inhaling deeply helps!

Homeplay

- ⚘ Often, as adults, we give and receive far more complaints (say five or more) for every one appreciation. For one day, try giving five appreciations (to yourself and others) before you make one complaint.
- ⚘ Try leading an interaction with appreciation. I (Philip) lead with appreciation when I write an e-mail message or meet someone. For example, in an e-mail, I might say, "I appreciate you for getting back to me so quickly." At the dry cleaner's, I might lead with an appreciation by saying, "I appreciate you for greeting me with a smile and for being so friendly."

APPENDIX

INFORMATION ON "SAFE SEX"

The SkyDancing Tantra vision is one that creates a healthier, more whole, and happier love life. This vision *does not* support behavior that is abusive, irresponsible, or enabling the transmission of diseases. Be absolutely certain that you enjoy healthy sex, not only while experimenting with SkyDancing Tantra skills in this workbook but also in your daily life.

To maintain your health and that of your partner, make safe sex a priority and understand what safe sex means. Information included in this workbook is only meant to give you some ideas. It is your responsibility to protect yourself in the best way to suit your lifestyle.

It is vital to communicate about safe sex with your partner, and to be clear with each other before you are close to practicing. Then your lovemaking can be free from any doubt and uncertainty, which would prevent you from being fully present and available for each other.

1. Tell each other your present sexual status, and of any past operations, and any diseases you have or might have, such as herpes, and where.
2. Share sexual histories, fears, desires, and questions, such as "Did you have unprotected sex with an unsafe partner?"
3. Communicate how together you will prevent sexual diseases from being transmitted and what form of birth control you choose to use, if needed.

This sharing can be touching, humorous, intimate, sobering, clearing, honest, and bring you closer to each other. This is one way of taking care of yourself and your own health that builds self-worth and self-love. You are empowered. You both know where you stand rather than going into sex blindly and uninformed, risking your health and future happiness for one spontaneous experience. Make a wise choice.

For additional information on safe sex,
read pages 429–435 of *The Art of Sexual Ecstasy.*
Also refer to *The Complete Guide to Safe Sex* by the Institute for
Advanced Study of Human Sexuality (Exodus Trust, 1992).

RESOURCES

After reading this book, you may be interested in attending a seminar that teaches these skills. For a current schedule and information on Margot Anand's new projects, including a DVD/video of *The Art of Sexual Ecstasy,* a companion to this book, contact:

Margot Anand Productions

20 Sunnyside Avenue, Suite A152

Mill Valley, CA 94941-1928

info@margotanandproductions.com

http://www.margotanandproductions.com and www.margotanand.com

Tel: 415-454-6030

The DVD/video includes detailed instruction from Margot, a demonstration of exercises, guided meditations, material from this book, and much more. It's like having Margot as your own private Tantra coach. (About 2 hours, 45 minutes long.)

To purchase Margot Anand's CDs *Sexual Breathing* (mentioned page 59) and *Music for Sensory Awakening* (mentioned page 89), contact Margot Anand Productions.

To purchase her music CDs *SkyDancing Tantra: A Call to Bliss* and *The Music of Everyday Ecstasy: Music for Passion, Spirit & Joy,* contact:

Spring Hill Media

1835 38th Street, Suite SW

Boulder, CO 80301

Tel: 303-938-1188; Fax: 303-938-1191

info@springhillmedia.com

http://www.springhillmedia.com

To purchase Margot Anand's audiocassette programs *The Art of Sexual Magic* and *Sexual Magic Meditations,* contact:

> Sounds True, Inc.
> 413 S. Arthur Avenue
> Louisville, CO 80027
> Tel: 303-665-3151
> Fax: 303-665-5292
> info@soundstrue.com
> http://www.soundstrue.com

To purchase Margot Anand's audio CD *The Art of Sexual Ecstasy,* which includes the Awakening the Inner Lover practice, contact:

> Inner Peace Music
> P.O. Box 2644
> San Anselmo, CA 94960
> Tel: 541-488-9424
> Fax: 541-488-7870
> innerpeace@wrightful.com
> http://www.stevenhalpern.com

To purchase Margot Anand's Pearls of Wisdom series, a compilation of her lectures, conferences, and interviews over the last fifteen years, contact:

> Margot Anand Productions
> 20 Sunnyside Avenue, Suite A152
> Mill Valley, CA 94941-1928
> info@margotanandproductions.com
> http://www.margotanandproductions.com

For the ideal "Tantra Holiday Experience in a Box," purchase Margot Anand's Kiss of Bliss Experience, a complete Tantra kit offering an exquisite tour of erotic delights. Contact: kissofbliss.com.

Other resources for ecstatic music and enlightened audio and video are:

New Earth Records
7 Avenida Vista Grande, Suite B7-305
Santa Fe, NM 87508
Tel: 505-466-2471; Fax: 505-466-2477
http://www.newearthrecords.com

Kahua Records
The Kahua Hawaiian Institute, LLC
P.O. Box 1747
Makawao, Maui, HI 96768
Tel: 808-572-6006; Fax: 808-572-0088
kahua@KahuaRecords.com
http://www.KahuaRecords.com

Music à la Carte
1111 Coolamon Scenic Drive
Mullumbimby, NSW 2482
Australia
Tel: 61-2-66843143; Fax: 61-2-66843144
customerservice@musicalacarte.net
http://www.musicalacarte.net

To purchase Awaken the Senses kits and *Awaken the Senses* CDs*, Dance the Three Keys to Orgasmic Power* music and activity CDs, *Stretch into Love* CDs with music by Shastro, and demonstration DVDs, as well as Philip's Tantric Stories series, books, and resources, contact:

Fun Unlimited, Inc.
Tel: 775-626-6634
Fax: 775-626-1228
info@fununlimitedinc.com
http://www.fununlimitedinc.com
and http://www.johncock.com

About the Authors

MARGOT ANAND is the bestselling author of *The Art of Sexual Ecstasy, The Art of Sexual Magic,* and *Sexual Ecstasy: The Art of Orgasm.* She developed SkyDancing Tantra, a path that has been taught successfully to more than forty thousand people internationally. She has conducted workshops, Love and Ecstasy Trainings, and SkyDancing Tantra Teacher Training programs at Esalen, the Omega Institute, Deepak Chopra's Center for Well-Being, the Tony Robbins "Ultimate Passion" couples' program at Namale in Fiji, and in SkyDancing Institutes in nine countries. Anand lives in northern California.

PHILIP DUANE JOHNCOCK is a multiuniversity grant-writing professor, social artist, and author of *Dream-Making to Billions: Grant Writing Tips from the Experts* and the Tantric Stories series. He is a licensed SkyDancing Tantra instructor, professional breath and movement trainer, and conscious relationship coach. Johncock lives in northern Nevada.